Taking the Go of Google My Business

15 Secrets

Directly From Google
to **Triple**
or Even **QUADRUPLE**
Your **MONEY** with
Your Google My Business Listing

Plus…

5 Tips

For Responding
To Negative Reviews
REVEALED

STEVE J HUSKEY

15-Point Google My Business Setup

1. Username (email address) and password for Google.

2. Website URL that you would like to link with your listing?

3. In 2 – 3 sentences, what makes your business unique? Is it 24/7 service? Quality of work? Or something else? Feel free to rewrite some text on your website. This is your description.

4. Include your 2 – 3 most lucrative services in the category fields. Try to use the Google auto populated categories here.

5. Use your company name on your business license or the sign outside your door. DO NOT improvise.

6. Mailing address.

7. How often do customers come to your business? If never, then do not list yourself as a service area

8. If yes, what is your physical address?

9. Include your main business phone number.

10. What is your main business email address?

11. What are the limits of your service areas? The northern-most, southern-most, eastern-most, and western-most limits?

12. What are your hours of operation?

13. List all forms of payment that you accept.

14. Include at least 5 photos. Photos of you and your staff will help soften your page. Be sure to designate one for your profile.

15. Is your map marker in the right place? Be sure to view both views: map and satellite.

Goo (g-u) is any viscous, sticky substance
Source: https://en.wikipedia.org/wiki/Goo

Goo slows you down.

Goo causes friction.

Goo impairs comprehension.

Do you want better results from Google?

In these easy-to-read pages, I equip you with methodologies that can make your listing show up above your competitors. I teach you how to turn FREE listings into powerful money-makers that help boost your Google rankings *fast*.

No special talents are necessary.

These methods cost nothing.

Once you read the tips,

It will be easy.

If you suffer from not having the knowledge or desire - as most business owners do today – this book will show you how to take the Goo out of Google. This will improve your Google My Business ranking.

Ready to dig in? Let's go!

Steve Huskey
a.k.a.: The Wizard of Google
Info@WizardOfGoogle.com
Twitter: @WizardOfGoogle
Website: http://www.winninggooglelocal.com/

PS – After reading this book, if you still need help, your first consultation is free.

Dedications

To my wife, for always going along with all of my new ideas.

To Cameron Tierney, whose dedication and personal instruction helped me land my first agency job in 2010.

Thank You.

Icons Used In This Book

 This icon will alert you to items that are particularly important.

 This icon is being used to signal information that you may want to write down for future reference.

 This icon gives you Google-approved advice.

Introduction

This is a business altering book. It will show you how to use Google My Business to get more traffic to your website. I am not exaggerating for effect. It is an absolute guarantee that if you read these principles, understand them, and then apply them, it will change your business in a fundamental way – for good.

Your business will have an improved public image. You will have more customers to harvest. You will be in more control of your future. Using these principles will significantly improve the quality of relationships with your customers. It will also improve the quantity of quality customers that find you. You can expect it, and it will happen. Once your listing gets ranked higher and your business gets noticed more, your capacity to inspire and persuade others will be enhanced. You will experience growth, learning, increased self-respect, self-confidence, and happiness. You can expect both dramatic and progressive results. This is an evolution not a revolution. This is not based on a fad or technique.

To make things increasingly easy, this book has been organized to follow a Google My Business listing setup from creation to completion. Once you complete a step with your online listing, simply turn the page in the book and you will be taken to the next step in the creation process. First, I will set expectations for how long this will take you from start to finish. I call it Google-time. It will be more closely defined in later chapters. Next, the setup is written in the same order as it will appears in Google's setup for easy reference. You will set it up according to how Google wants an effective listing to read.

As quickly as you can turn the page, you can setup your listing. Finally, we go through trouble shooting common issues and their fixes.

Don't forget to pay attention to the notification icons. There are three icons that highlight particularly important pieces of information. Simply paying attention to these will take some of the goo out of your Google My Business set up.

This book is a compilation of the presentations I have attended, my continuing education online, and real work experiences as a professional internet marketing consultant. What I learned is that it is Google's interpretation of our listing that affects our ranking.

These methodologies apply to large businesses, small businesses, non-profits, startups, private businesses, and Fortune 500 companies. They are like common denominators. They are principles that apply to everyone using Google.

Most people tend to want a quick fix. Many online marketing professionals give quick promises of relief. The difficulty is they work on acute issues or problems without looking at the big picture. They want your pain to be relieved instantly so that relationship can be instantly formed. They are into tricks. The more you try to apply a gimmick or quick fix, the worse your problems may become.

These methodologies address the chronic problems and expose opportunities.

Google Wants to do Business with You

When was the last time you got something for free? Every time you use Google, you are using a free service. Google doesn't own much of what you want. They are the broker for what you want.

Google's mission statement reads, "To organize the world's information and make it universally accessible and useful." To do this they count on you the business owner to help them out. It is in your best interest to list your business, but it is also in Google's best interest that you list your information. So be patient and know they are just as enthusiastic to have your information indexed as you are. They want to broker the information. They just want to check your credentials and credibility first.

Speaking of brokers, if you have used a broker for free, how was the quality of their work? Likely if their service was free, you got what you paid for. Did they let you use their service for free again and again, as often as you liked?

Google strives to give you the most recent, relevant information that you are looking for. This is so much more than a phone book. It is an encyclopedia, almanac, map, meteorologist, email service, video database, and all around information broker. It does all of these things repeatedly for free. Best of all, they are constantly striving to serve you better.

One of the ways they do this is by using something they call Quality Score. It's Google's way of separating websites that are relevant to your search term from those that are not. The factors include, website quality, website load time, and how often people click on your listing when it is shown, (a.k.a. click through rate).

Google monitors quality score with special software robots that crawl the web looking for new information. These are also called spiders. By taking note of the words on a page and where they were found, Google is able to assign a site a quality score. This, in turn, helps them show you a relevant result. By showing you a more relevant result on your first try, the idea is that you'll come back to Google to search again.

The Phone Book is Dead!

Google My Business (a.k.a. Google Local, Google Places, or Google Maps) connects searchers with relevant local listings on the map. Google's annual report says they have more than 50 million map listings worldwide. This service has proven so popular that it is now featured in the top right corner of most searches. When people want to find a local business, it is faster and easier than ever to see how far they are from a business using the map. Surfers can see details about your business including pictures and videos. Best of all, it's free!

There is no reason why your business should not be on the first page of Google…unless you're not interested in profitability. Google wants you to be there. Google will list you for free *if* you follow its rules. Rule #1, have your page filled out entirely - 100%. Getting to 100% is a matter of filling out all of the information in the format Google wants.

Rule #2, Google wants fresh and relevant information for its users. It is important to keep your page fresh with new content. Content consists of pictures, videos, reviews, etc… Add something new every 21 days-ish.

Bottom line: Complete the steps in this book and you will make more money.

Give Google My Business Your Full Attention

What do you mean give Google My Business my full attention? Are you crazy?

I have found that taking the path of least resistance with Google will help your page get ranked faster and more consistently. If you want to be liked by Google, you must work with them - on their terms. Again, Google is a huge public company. They are not required to list your business in their database. Therefore, following what they say will pay dividends; your listing will be shown more often, for more keywords, and in better placement. Failing to follow this, will most often get your page marked as spam and likely delisted from Google. More on this spam later.

Unless you are an Internet marketing manager, you may not have noticed that Google Local, formerly Google Places, Google Maps, is now Google My Business. Though, in the setup, Google still mentions "my maps listing". Gone is the Zagat-esque method of reviews, which gives options to select between 0 and 3 stars. Google has re-adopted a 1 – 5 star review method. They found that the 5 star review system worked well across all industries. The review is weighted based on the number of reviews that you have. For example, if you only have two 5 star reviews, does that mean that you deserve 5.0 stars? What about a business that has 75 reviews that range from 60% 5 stars, 30% 4 stars and 10% 3 stars or less. Does that mean that your two reviews is better than their 75 review? Google doesn't think so. Google would likely reward the business with 2 reviews a score of 4.3 ish and the business with 75 reviews would likely get the average of their score. Google thinks the business with 75 reviews is more relevant and will reward them.

Further changes have integrated Google My Business with Menu.com and OpenTable.com for reservations and menus respectively. Looking for a new restaurant? You're now able to look at the menu and reserve a table with help from the Google My Business interface.

Do you know how to get more reviews?

Stay tuned. We will cover that in detail later in the book.

What is Google Time?

One of the major frustrations I hear from customers is the time required to make these changes. Remember that Google is a massive public company. They can do what they want. If you want to be seen on Google, you must remember that you are not dealing with a standardized time zone. You are effectively progressing on Google time.

Google does not push out all the information it has in real time. Google time does not work on a 24-hour clock; it functions through periodic index pushes. Often times an index push will take 3 – 4 weeks before a server will be refreshed. If your changes have taken more than 45 days, then it might be time to redo the changes. Essentially, this "pokes" Google in asking for an update. However, Google's own literature will tell you that they can take up to 30 days to process any changes. When you add that to a potential 3-week lag time for an index push, you could easily be looking at 51 days of turnaround time.

Google is trying to weed out companies that are relevant from those that are trying to appear relevant. In doing so their rankings are always evolving.

So give your attention to your Google My Business listing. It will bring more customers to your business once it's 100% complete.

How to Setup Google My Business

Step 1 – Sign in to your Google account to start the process

1) Search for the business using the name and address.
2) Click "Be the first to review" or "review" which will take you to the Google My Business page. If the review window pops up, hit "cancel".
3) If it asks you if I'm authorized – check "yes"
4) Verify authorization from Google either by mail or phone. Phone will happen immediately. Be ready.

If you need Google to send a confirmation, get the verification code delivered by text.

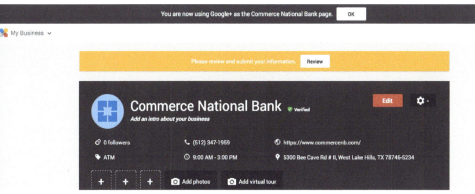

Google My Business Profile after verification

5) Go to settings
Check everything
Add your name as the contact, press enter
Go through the verification process

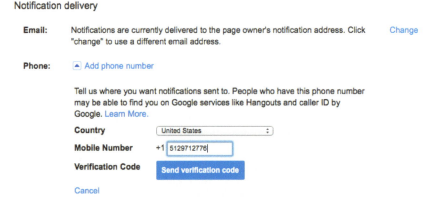

Google My Business Notification Delivery

6) Go to Managers
   Verify my ownership
7) Fill out profile. More detailed information can be found on
   the pages following this setup.
   a) Intro: must be a sentence or Google may classify as your
      Google My Business profile as spam

 Change intro to reflect high impression keywords found in Google Adwords or Analytics

When done, go to Google+ (found on left hand side of page under Google My Business button)

8) Go to videos and upload video. This will force you to create a YouTube profile
9) Click on "Pages" (left hand side), manage this page/settings.
10) Click on "Create a new page" to claim pages/profiles

Basic Information

I f you have a Gmail or a Google account for your business, then your best bet is to log-in with that. You can use that Gmail or Google account as your Google My Business account. If you do not have a Gmail or a Google account, then go set one up.

Go to www.Gmail.com and click "set up a new Gmail account". You do not ever have to actually use it as an email, but that can be your Google log-in. Next, log-in with your email address. It will take you to https://www.google.com/business/. Scroll down until you see "Get your business found on Google". Now click "Get started." It will ask you to log-in.

If you DO NOT already have a Google My Business page associated with the account, the setup interface will bring you to a separate window. If you DO have a Google My Business page associated with that email, it is going to bring you directly to the dashboard.

Just because you did not create it does not mean that it has not already been created for you.

Now look for your page. Try typing in your business address. If there is a Google My Business page under that address, then a Google My Business page was already created for this. Now click the "Manage This Page" button. It is going to allow you to edit that information then submit and verify it. In the instance that you no longer have access to the log-in information for the email address tied to your Google account, you can log-in with the Gmail account that you just created. Unfortunately, you will have to put in the business phone number, and then click the "Edit" button. Then you must go through the verification process yet again. This is Google's way of securely transferring the ownership from the old page to the new page. The bottom line is, clicking the "Edit" button will walk you to the process to re-verify it under a new email address.

If you do have a duplicate page, go to my section on troubleshooting for tips on dealing with this.

If you DO NOT have a Google My Business page created for you already, you will have a blank slate. This is your opportunity to go through and fill out all the information.

 Don't just fill out the information that's required. Fill out every single field. Ideally your target should be to get your account to 100% completeness.

How do you know if you are at 100%? When you log in to "Edit This Business Listing", under "Business Info", there is a scrubber bar that tells you the percentage towards complete that you are. This long blue bar is located on your page. It will tell you the percentage complete. This needs to be at a 100%. If it's not, then you are not ranking as high as you could and possibly not showing at all. Rarely do I see a Google listing that has 100% completeness. It is an easy thing to do. You just have to take the time to do it. You will need several pieces of basic information. For example:

- company name on your sign or business license
- physical address
- phone number
- email address
- website

 It is widely thought that Google sorts their databases by phone number. Using a consistent phone number on all of your Google pages and other directory listings will have an impact on how well your Google My Business listing ranks.

Google Insiders say: Some of the ranking of your Google My Business listing has to do with the Search Engine Optimization (SEO) of the website that is linked to the listing.

If there is a website linked to the Google My Business page, you can bet that Google's spiders are indexing it and correlating the information. This gives Google a better picture of the business.

Once you gather all of the above information, you're ready to start.

Description

Always fill out the description area knowing that it is keyword-sensitive. A good tactic is to have this area full of keywords weaved into sentences. This is one of the first things that people are going to read. What is the single biggest benefit to doing business with you vs one of your competitors? Put it here

Ensure that visitors can see what the company offers in the description field. Visitors will see your description field.

Many people get the description and category fields confused. They serve two different purposes. The description field is telling consumers what the company is all about. If there are services not listed in the auto populated categories, list them in the description field.

You should add up to 3 keywords. For example, our services include, A, B, and C.

Categories

The category field is telling Google where this page should show up. Though visitors can see the categories, many times they are truncated, which means, visitors will only see the first one.

This is also a futuristic tool for semantic search. In the very near future, you will be able into speak to your phone about what you want. Instead of going to a search engine and typing in, "Dallas private scuba diving lessons", you'll be able to speak into your phone saying "Dallas scuba diving instructor". It's called semantic search and it will change the way we search the internet. Google has setup the category field in advance of the semantic search phenomenon.

Regardless, the rule is to always fill out as many auto populated categories as apply. <u>One of those must be a designated auto populated category</u>. For example, when you start typing in "scuba", the category "dive shop" will auto-populate. It is a pre-set category. You must have one true Google category.

The Most Important Detail to Remember When Setting up a Category

Remember, this is all about semantic search. It has to fit into the following statement; "this place is a (insert description here)".Google is specifically looking for the category keywords to be structured in this way. For example, you would not say "this place is a scuba dive". You would say "this place is a scuba diving instructor", or "this place scuba rental shop" or "this place is a swim lessons center". This is incredibly important because if you do not fit into

Google's particular phrasing, it could be marked as category spam. Worse yet, their software might misinterpret your page.

Bottom line: try to choose categories that are auto-populated.

In my experience, 9 times out of 10, when a page is not showing it is due to category spam.

Service Areas and Location Settings

How to Hide Your Address

This can be a big issue for businesses that do not want the potential harassment from customers. If you work at home or have a business that just has a P.O. Box and no physical store front, then list the address where you receive mail. Often that is the home address.

"But I don't want my address to show up on the map", you say. If you do not want your address to show up then click, "Service Area". Next, click the check box, "I service customers at their location". It's a great strategy for the businesses that work at the customer's site like plumbers, locksmiths, and HVAC. This will also help home businesses that do not want customers showing up at their home during dinner time.

Now you can offer a custom service area. For example, the service area for your company could be a 20-mile radius from an individual zip code, or you could choose a city. The Google interface will create a service area for you.

 The Google My Business pages that perform the best have a physical address listed. The reason being, Google My Business is designed to help people connect with local businesses.

Some Categories Give You Secret Access

Below is a screenshot for a magazine publisher. After following the setup guide listed in this book, he was able to list all of the drop points in Google's map interface. Now, when searching for the magazine, this is what shows up.

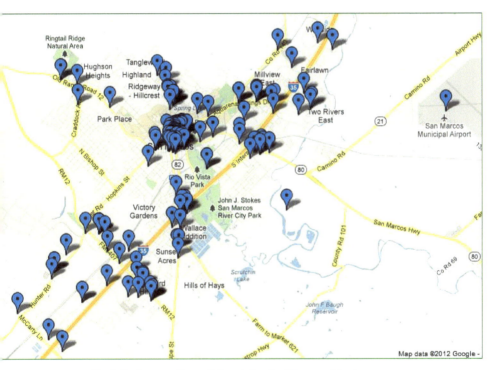

Publishers Can List Their Drop Points

Google My Business Hours of Operation

You Are Always Open

Business Hours: Sometimes I hear from people that there are not operating hours for their business. Understandably, not all businesses have operating hours. Nonetheless, if your business has hours, it is essential that you include them in the Google My Business setup. It is extremely important now because there is an option in the mobile app that says, "Only show me businesses that are open now." The bottom line, if you do not have hours listed, then your listing is not going to show up.

Sign Up Today

30-Day Money-Back Guarantee

Photos and Videos

A dding photos and videos is simple. To do this, simply click "Add Photo" or "Add video". Find them on your computer and upload them into the Google My Business interface. Or you can link to any YouTube video that you have the rights to. Use these to communicate the culture and the services.

Photos and videos add more depth to the page and the click through rates are better.

Ideas for photos include: office view from the street, smiling staff members, staff members at work, staff members collaborating with one another or the owners, vehicle with logo on it, or business pet. This part of the page is one of the biggest factors in success. There is a correlation between more pictures and more activity.

Don't link to a video that you don't have permission to. If it gets flagged, it will cause the Google My Business listing to be pulled down.

Once you've completed these steps, you will be able to verify the listing by phone or mail. The postcard listing

Hello from Google,

You're almost done registering your business with Google.

After you verify your identity, your listing will go live in about a day. Then you can easily:

- Keep your hours, website, and other details up to date.
- Stand out with photos, videos, even coupons.
- View your personalized business dashboard for stats on who's visiting your listing and requesting directions to you.

Customers like to know what's going on right now. Log in frequently to keep your information current and to check your latest stats on your business dashboard.

Your business listing is:

Dr. Seuss
4407 Your Street
West Urban Area
TX
78 123

To verify your identity:

Step 1:
Go to www.google.com/local/add

Step 2:
To sign in, use your password and Google Account ID

Step 3:
Enter your PIN in the field next to your business listing and click **Go.**

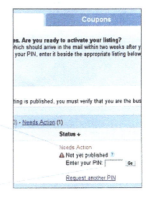

Your Pin is: **12345**

For more information, click "Google Places Help" at the bottom of **www.google.com/local/add**

Duplicate Pages

I f you have duplicate pages and have tried to remove some/all of them, but still continue to see the old page, it could be a matter of timing. For example, some of the pages could still be cached somewhere on a server that you have no control over. Until a new index push is created, your old version of the page will not be erased. In a situation where there are duplicate pages and many of them share the same address, the server is trying to cluster the pages all together.

This has created a confusing situation for Google's computers. It is a known issue and Google is working on it. Remember, we are working on Google time. Google's policy gives them 30 days to respond to a review. They try to do an index push every 3 weeks. This means that a normal response time could be as long as 51 days.

You could also have multiple listings in the same Google My Business Dashboard for the same business location. If this is the case it is recommended that you make sure you have all the content backed up from the listing you will keep. Make sure the listing you want to keep is "active". Your best bet for success here is to fill out the "contact me" form and let Google walk you through this by phone.

If none of those options work. Call us. We can help.

Google My Business Troubleshooting

My listing is not showing as frequently as I would like.

Brand new listings sometimes will have a 90-day period during which the listing will not be shown in the regular rotation. Google wants to ensure sure that this is a legitimate business, that this information is correct.

What can I do to get into the rotation more?

First, make sure your page is 100% complete. Has it been complete for 90 days? Google will give you page a 90-day demotion period while it evaluates your authenticity. Can you blame them? They want to ensure that illegitimate business pages like that don't get ranked.

Second, are your categories and description properly filled out? If not, you could be marked for category spam.

 Do not add anything to the company name that is different from what reads on your business license.

As a general rule, you cannot have anything in the company organization field that is not exactly how it reads on the sign on your door, on your business cards, and on your business license. The same applies to your address.

Third, on the second address line, many businesses have included things like "best dive shop in Miami", or "biggest store on rodeo drive", or "the big blue store at sun ridge mall. I have even seen people try to put keywords in this field. This is spam.

My map marker is not in the correct place

Log into your Google My Business account. Go to the user interface indicated by an icon that says "Business Owner". Click on "edit my page". Underneath the map, click on "Fix Incorrect Marker Location." Scroll up to the top. That will open a dynamic window that allows you to literally pick up the map marker and move it. Now click "save changes". Scroll back down to the bottom and click "submit". Your map marker has been changed.

I did everything you said and I'm still not showing

Did you wait 60 days? Remember, Google's literature shows that a 51 day response time is normal. Often times, a change will reflect on the back-end server, but will not be pushed to the live server until Google has a large index push. Google is trying to do a new push every 3-4 weeks.

Try giving it 60 days, if it still doesn't rank, call me. I will be happy to give you a free consultation.

Reviews

Having reviews is powerful. It not only provides more text for Google spiders to crawl, but often reviews are SEO-rich because customers are talking about the services that they had at your office.

As mentioned earlier, the reviews have recently changed in an incredible way. Now, when you're signed into Google and looking for a review, Google will show you reviews from people you know first. Obviously, you're going to tend to believe a review from someone you know as opposed to someone you aren't familiar with. You trust the people you're interacting with more. This is only going to grow in importance.

So not only are reviews one of the most important factors for your business, but they will continue to grow in importance in the future. Bottom line: get more reviews on your Google My Business page.

A Google My Business listing with 5 reviews will show up in search results.

To capture more reviews, a recommended strategy is to have a Google My Business badge on your website that links to your Google page. Somewhere around the icon, in text, you could say "Tell us about your experience". Again, that icon should link directly to the Google My Business page where they can write a review. You can also hand out business cards that have a photo of your business on one side and on the other side say, "Were we friendly? Tell us about it."

Driving traffic to the Google My Business page and getting customers to select the star ratings is fine. For your customers to write a fully-developed idea of what they thought the business was, what they thought could be done better, and what they love about it will give your Google My Business page a better ranking. Conversely, if the passion that you have for your business shows through in responding to a negative review, it is exponentially more valuable for future potential customers to see that than it is to have somebody put a 5-star review that says, "Food is great."

Responding to Negative Reviews is Easy

What to say?
What to avoid saying?
Who are you writing to?

If your response includes too many keywords your review response may be ranked as quality content. You certainly do not want to bring any more attention to the negative review.

First, understand that you are *not* talking to the person who wrote the review. You are talking to potential customers who may be reading the review later.

An owner can (and should) respond to reviews. Within the Google dashboard, there is a tab that says "Respond to reviews." Click it. Now you can scroll down to all of the reviews and respond publicly as the owner. Use this simple checklist below.

5-Point Checklist to Respond to Reviews

Quite often, business owners call me asking, "How can I remove a negative review?" Removing that review is nearly impossible. The best thing that you can do is to respond to the review. Again, remember your audience. You are not talking to the person who wrote the review, you are talking to the future customers who will be making a decision about your business while reading the review. Use the following points to help you craft a solid response.

1. Is the review true?
2. If yes, what did you do to rectify the issue?
3. If no, what makes you think it is untrue?
4. If this happened today, what would be different?
5. Ask a neutral party to read the response to ensure it's unemotional.

Everyone makes mistakes. Everyone has customers that they just can't keep happy. If you follow this checklist, your reviews will look like they were written by a customer service pro.

When responding to a review, keywords are weighted heavily. Try to use as few keywords as possible.

You've Got Your Page Set Up, Now What?

The first thing you need to do is familiarize yourself with the Google + dashboard.

 Save it on your favorites so that you can come back to create and schedule your posts

This can be done from plus.google.com/dashboard. Once you get to the dashboard, go to "Share New" box. The "Share New" section is where you are able to schedule your posts. In the posts, you can make it an easy as entering in content that is already on your website. For the best results you should do this every 21 days (more than once a month). Google My Business does not rank on a 30 day cycle, they are looking for activity. If you are active at least every 21 days, you will rank higher on Google's activity scale.

Pictures

Your page needs lots of pictures. Google is requesting more images and are now allowing interior, exterior, and staff pictures. Add as many as you can to your page.

Before you upload your images to Google, make sure to label all of your images with keywords.

Google's interface is great because they automatically bring up what they think is the best fit right off the bat. You can either choose the one that Google has picked, or cycle through the others and choose which one you prefer.

Links

Link to various pages on your website. When linking, use the content from the page in the post. For example, do not link to your "About Us" page and include content from your "Services" page. Instead, link to the "Services" page and use content from the "Services" page. You are not required to add videos. However, Google will consider your page more active every time you link to a public video on YouTube. If you do not link to it, you can "like" a video on YouTube or save it to your favorites, it will show up on Google + in your activity stream.

Follows

It is important to Google that you are an active member of their online community. To make your page more active without helping your competitors, you want to follow people in your industry and those that are relevant to your industry. If you are a doctor's office, it is not as valuable to your ranking if you follow a seafood restaurant. You need to follow people / organizations that are relevant to the medical industry.

The way you do this is to find people with similar occupations in other cities. These people should not be competitors.

If your office is in Dallas, do not follow someone in Fort Worth. If you're in Texas, you may want to search for some of your colleagues in California, Arizona, or Florida. Search for relevant companies or people in your industry in other places and follow them – it will increase your activity level on Google.

The best practice for increasing your activity level on Google is follow 12-15 new people monthly. You can do this all at the same time, but sporadically is better. Some of these people will inevitably follow you in return.

+1's or Likes

Something else Google My Business is looking for in ranking your Google My Business page is "+1's", which is the most simple to do. It is easy when you "+1" something to post a comment too. Go find some industry relevant content and like / comment on it.

DO NOT like or comment on any posts or content from your competitors.

You need to "like" posts from people in other cities, other areas, other countries even. Follow people in Spain, Europe, or Mexico! Just do not follow your competitors.

Getting Return Responses

When you are commenting on other's posts, if you want to get a return response you can try posing a question. Some easy questions to ask that get return responses are:

"What do you have planned next?"

"What are you doing next year?"

"Are there any other projects you're working on?"

I find that asking them "what's next" invokes a passionate response. They may be willing to brag about little secrets. That is good content and it shows Google that you are being active. You do not have to respond. Just the fact that they responded to you gives you bonus points.

Fans/ Followers

Of course, you want to get fans and followers. Using the response technique will build your followers quickly.

Remember that Google My Business is Google's most clicked on feature from a desktop and from a mobile device. Currently, people with Android mobile devices occupy an 80% market share worldwide. Android comes with Google Maps as the standard interface for that device. So 80% of the world's population is going to use it. It is free. It is not easy to control, but you can get your listing shown 7-10 times more frequently in front of people who are in your local area and have just typed in a term that is relevant to your business. Currently, there is no better form of free advertising on Google.

If you need help with your Google My Business page, contact us today for a free consultation.

Closing

Believe it or not, you know more about creating an effective Google listing than the majority of your competitors. The tips and methodologies I've shared with you in Taking the Goo Out of Google My Business are the same that online marketing consultants would use if you paid them 50 times the amount you paid for this book. Now you can use them yourself and reap the benefits.

Remember, the secret is to ensure your listing setup is 100% complete - in a way that Google can read it.

I'm sincerely appreciative of the interest you've expressed by reading this book.

To request a free consultation or additional information about High 5 Promotion's online marketing programs or other products and services, please call 512.200.2295. You can also email Info@WizardOfGoogle.com or visit us online http://www.winninggooglelocal.com/.

Please let us know how the ideas in this book have helped you by reviewing us at https://plus.google.com/+WizardofGoogleAustin/posts

Thanks.

www.ingramcontent.com/pod-product-compliance
Lightning Source LLC
Chambersburg PA
CBHW041938080326
R17960000001B/R179600PG40689CBX00002B/3